DIANA, *Princess of Wales*

by Carol Greene

CHILDRENS PRESS, CHICAGO®

Picture Acknowledgements

British Information Service—Cover, 20, 30

United Press International—2, 6, 21 (right), 22 (right), 24, 25, 26, 29

Wide World Photos—8 (left), 17, 23, 31 (left)

Syndication International/Photo Trends—8 (top right), 8 (bottom right), 9, 10, 11, 12, 13, 15, 16, 18, 19, 21 (left), 22 (left), 23, 31 (right)

Camera Press/Photo Trends—8 (center)
Snowdon/Camera Press/Photo Trends—32

Library of Congress Cataloging in Publication Data

Greene, Carol.
  Diana, Princess of Wales.

  (Picture-story biographies)

  Summary: Describes the childhood, wedding, and work
of Lady Diana, who married Prince Charles of England and
became Princess of Wales.
  1. Diana, Princess of Wales, 1961- —Juvenile literature.
2. Great Britain—Princess and princesses—Biography—
Juvenile literature. [1. Diana, Princess of Wales, 1961-
2. Princesses] I. Title.
DA591.A45D5315   1985   941.085'092'4 [B] [92]   85-12751
ISBN 0-516-03538-X

7/87 10.60 BD · CT

DIANA, Princess of Wales

People everywhere know Diana. They like to read about her. They like to look at pictures of her. Some even try to dress the way she does.

What's so special about Diana? She's a princess. She is married to Charles, the Prince of Wales. That makes Diana the Princess of Wales. Someday she may be the queen of England. That's special!

Of course, her family didn't know any of that when Diana was born on July 1, 1961. The Spencers thought she simply was another daughter. They already had two. Sarah was six when Diana was born and Jane was four. This time the Spencers had wanted a boy. But they got Diana— and they loved her.

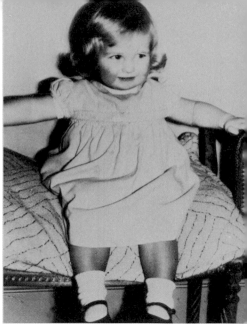

The Royal Family at Windsor Castle in 1968. Seated from left to right: Prince Philip, Prince Edward, Queen Elizabeth. Standing: Princess Anne, Prince Charles, Prince Andrew. (Opposite page) Diana's parents at their wedding, 1954. Diana (top left), Prince Edward, and Prince Andrew.

The Spencer home was called Park House. It was on a big piece of land called Sandringham. England's royal family owned Sandringham. Sometimes they stayed in another house there. Then the Spencer children could play with the little princes, Andrew and Edward.

When Diana was almost three, her brother Charles was born. Diana loved to take care of him. She could hardly wait for his baptism. It would be in a huge church called Westminster Abbey, in London. But the day before the baptism, Diana fell down some steps and bruised her head. So she couldn't go after all.

When she was four, Diana began to have school lessons at home with her big sisters. A governess, Gertrude Allen, taught them. The children called her Ally.

Four-year-old Diana with her brother, Charles.

Rare pictures from the Spencer family photo album capture the shy side of Diana.

Then, when Diana was six, her sisters went away to boarding school. Ally left, too. So did Diana's nanny, the woman who took care of her. Worst of all, her mother went away. She and Diana's father were not happy with each other any more. After a while, they got a divorce.

All this made Diana very unhappy. Sometimes she cried. Sometimes she got angry. But she tried to keep busy. Then she didn't think about her problems so much.

At last, Diana's father decided that she and her brother should go to a regular school. He sent them to Silfield School. Diana loved it. She was a good reader and she wrote well, too. But she liked helping the smaller children best.

Her father knew that Diana was trying hard at school. He wanted to reward her. So for her seventh birthday party, he borrowed a camel from a zoo. All the children at the party got to ride it.

Diana was an average student—one of many at Riddlesworth Hall. She is the one with pigtails in front of the sixth girl from the left in the back row.

That fall, Diana went away to a boarding school called Riddlesworth Hall. It wasn't too far from Park House. There was plenty of work to do. But there was also time for fun. Each girl at Riddlesworth could have a small pet. Diana had a guinea pig called Peanuts.

Diana spent part of her vacations with her father at Park House. She spent the rest with her mother and her mother's new husband, Peter Shand Kydd. Diana liked him.

Diana stayed at Riddlesworth Hall until she was twelve. She was never the smartest girl in her class. But she loved swimming, ballet, and helping other people. She even won a school award for being so helpful.

In 1973, Diana went to another boarding school, West Heath. Again her favorite subjects were swimming and dancing. She won awards in both. But she still liked working with children. Maybe she would do that when she left school.

Her mother and stepfather had moved to an island off the coast of Scotland. So Diana had a new place to go on vacations. Her mother raised Shetland ponies and Diana helped her with them.

The headmistress at the exclusive West Heath boarding school
remembers Diana as "a girl who noticed what needed to be done and
then did it willingly and cheerfully."

Diana shared a dormitory with other girls
at West Heath. She kept a photo of
Prince Charles above her bed. During
some school holidays, Diana (right)
visited her mother in Scotland.

The Spencer family. From left to right: Sarah, Diana, Charles, their stepmother Raine with her mother, novelist Barbara Cartland, and Jane.

Sometimes, though, she spent weekends with her sisters in London. Then she liked to wash their clothes and clean up their apartments. Diana thought cleaning was fun.

In 1975, her life changed again. Her grandfather died and her father became an earl. That meant that Diana was now officially Lady Diana. It also meant that her father had to move to the official family home at Althorp. Diana never liked that house. It was too big.

In 1978 Diana's sister, Jane, married Mr. Robert Fellowes. Diana was her bridesmaid. Her mother and father (above), her older sister Sarah, and her stepmother (far left) attended the wedding.

In 1977, Diana left West Heath. Her parents thought she might like another school in Switzerland. But she didn't. After a few weeks, she left it and moved in with her mother in London.

17

Meanwhile, something very exciting had happened to Diana. Her sister Sarah had brought a friend to Althorp. Diana met him there. His name was Charles and he was the Prince of Wales, son of the queen of England and older brother of Diana's royal playmates, Andrew and Edward. Later Diana said she thought Charles was "pretty amazing." She couldn't help thinking about him sometimes after that.

Friends with whom Diana shared her London apartment knew that she would one day marry Prince Charles.

Shortly after her eighteenth birthday, Diana's parents bought her a three-bedroom flat at 60 Coleherne Court, London, and a car.

But now she had to decide what to do with her life. She lived with some other girls in London. That was fun. But she wanted to work, too.

So, first she did baby-sitting and cleaning jobs. Then she took a cooking course. Next she wanted to teach dancing to children. But none of these was just right.

At last, in the fall of 1979, Diana
found the perfect job. She became
an assistant at the Young England
Kindergarten. She loved the children
and they loved her.

She still thought a lot about Charles, though. She had met him again at a party at Sandringham. After that, he asked her out. Would she like to go to the ballet with him and his friends? How about the opera? Of course she would!

Charles and Diana at a Scottish hideaway (left) and at a benefit concert in London (right).

Not long after Diana accompanied Charles to a polo match, they announced their engagement at Buckingham Palace.

But Charles didn't get serious until the summer of 1980. Then he asked her to watch him play polo. Next he invited her to a ball. After that came a party on the royal yacht.

After a while, newspaper people noticed what was happening. Soon they followed Diana everywhere. How did she feel about Charles? How did he feel about her?

Diana tried to be polite to the reporters. But sometimes they pushed too hard. Once she had to climb over trash cans to get away from them. Other times they printed stories that weren't true. Those stories upset Diana. They made Charles angry.

At last, on February 5, 1981, Charles invited Diana to have dinner with him at Buckingham Palace. While she was there, he asked her to marry him. She said yes.

The royal family was delighted. They thought Diana was just right for Charles. On February 24 Charles's parents, Queen Elizabeth and Prince Philip, officially announced the engagement. The British government cheered. Prince Charles's ship fired a twenty-one-gun salute. Letters and telegrams poured in from all over the world.

Queen Elizabeth announced with "the greatest pleasure" the engagement of her son to Lady Diana Spencer. Charles was 32. Diana was 19.

Now Diana had a big job ahead of her. She had to get ready for a royal wedding.

She moved into Buckingham Palace. There she had plenty of people to help her. Together they planned the wedding, bought clothes, and wrote thank-you notes. (Charles and Diana were given over ten thousand presents.) Then there were parties, dinners, and interviews.

Millions of people watched the fairy tale wedding of Prince Charles and Lady Diana. She arrived at the cathedral in a Glass Coach and walked down the aisle in silk slippers.

But at last Diana woke up to her wedding day, Wednesday, July 29, 1981. The ceremony was at Saint Paul's Cathedral in London. Kings, queens, presidents, and prime ministers waited in the cathedral. So did Diana's friends. Over a million people lined the streets. Seven hundred million watched on TV.

At 11:00 A.M., Diana walked down the aisle. She wore an ivory-colored dress with pearls, lace, bows, and a twenty-five-foot train. She carried a bouquet with orchids and golden roses. On her finger she wore her engagement ring, a blue sapphire with fourteen diamonds around it.

The archbishop of Canterbury
married Charles and Diana. He said
this day was just the beginning of
their adventure. He was right.

When Diana left the cathedral,
she was Princess of Wales. From
now on, she would travel all over the
world and meet many people.

The christening of Prince William took place in Buckingham Palace.
The Queen Mother (right) posed proudly.

Princess Diana has done a fine
job of that. She has always been
good at getting along with people.
She still likes to help them. She
works for a school for the blind, a
cancer fund for children, a preschool
group, and other charities.

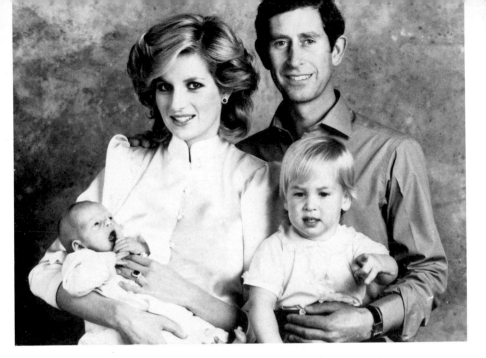

Once a shy little girl, Diana now assumes the roles
of princess and wife and mother of a future king.

Diana and Charles now have two children. Prince William was born on June 21, 1982. Prince Henry (called Harry) arrived on September 15, 1984. Diana wants to be a good mother. She tries to be with her children as much as she can.

Sometimes Diana must remember when *she* was a child. She was just another little girl then. But amazing things can happen in this world. And today Diana is a princess.

Diana, Princess of Wales

1961	July 1—Born at Park House, Norfolk, England, third daughter of Edward John and Frances Spencer
1967	Parents separated
1968-70	Attended Silfield School, King's Lynn
1969	Mother married Peter Shand Kydd
1970-73	Attended Riddlesworth Hall, Norfolk
1973-77	Attended West Heath, Kent
1975	Became Lady Diana Spencer
1976	Father married Raine, Countess of Dartmouth
1977	Met Charles, Prince of Wales, at Althorp
1978-81	Lived and worked in London
1981	February 5—Prince Charles proposed
	February 24—Engagement officially announced
	July 29—Married Charles, Prince of Wales
1982	June 21—Prince William born
1984	September 15—Prince Henry (Harry) born

ABOUT THE AUTHOR

CAROL GREENE has degrees in English Literature and Musicology. She has worked in international exchange programs, as an editor and as a teacher. She now lives in Saint Louis, Missouri, and writes full-time. She has published over fifty books—most of them for children. Other Childrens Press biographies by Ms. Greene include *Sandra Day O'Connor: First Woman on the Supreme Court*, *Mother Teresa: Friend of the Friendless*, and *Indira Gandhi* in the Picture Story Biography series, and *Louisa May Alcott, Marie Curie,* and *Thomas Alva Edison* in the People of Distinction series.